Presented to

Sadie MacIllvarth

By

Portree Parish

Sunday School

2015

"Great is the Lord and greatly to be
praised" Psalm 48:1

you will
show me the path
of light: in
your presence
is fullness of joy

For my Mum and Dad
Heather Stuart

**Published by**
**The Bible Reading Fellowship**
15 The Chambers, Vineyard
Abingdon, OX14 3FE
United Kingdom
Tel: +44 (0)1865 319700
Email: enquiries@brf.org.uk
Website: www.brf.org.uk
BRF is a Registered Charity
ISBN 978 1 84101 820 1
First edition 2011

Publishing Director: Annette Reynolds
Art Director: Gerald Rogers
Pre-production Manager: Krystyna Kowalska Hewitt
Production Manager: John Laister

Printed and bound in Singapore

# BARNABAS
# CHILDREN'S
# PRAYERS

Compiled and written by Bethan James

Illustrated by Heather Stuart

# Contents

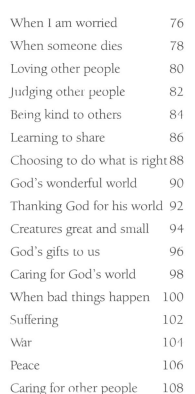

1

Our Father in heaven,
hallowed be your name.
Your kingdom come,
your will be done,
on earth as in heaven.
Give us today our daily bread.
Forgive us our sins,
as we forgive those who sin against us.
Lead us not into temptation,
but deliver us from evil.
For the kingdom,
the power and the glory are yours.
Now and for ever. Amen

BASED ON MATTHEW 6:10–14

2

Father God,
may your kingdom come
every day, every way.
May there be peace and happiness,
love and joy and friends,
quarrels forgotten,
healing for hurting,
sunshine and stars
for sad, shadowy skies.
Come into our world,
come into our towns,
come into our homes.
Amen

JAN GODFREY

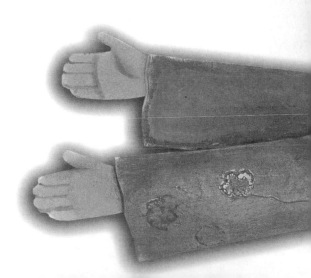

### 3

Still, still, Jesus is here.
Hush, hush, angels are near.
Open my ears, Lord, help me to hear
your voice in the stillness.

ROSEMARY CARPENTER

### 4

I don't know how to pray, Lord.
Please help me!

BEN, AGED 5

### 5

Lord God, you know when I wake up
and you know when I go to sleep.
Thank you that you are always here.

BETHAN JAMES

6

We bow our heads
And close our eyes
Before we start to pray.
Thank you, God, for listening
To every word we say.

BASED ON A PRAYER FROM THE PHILIPPINES

7

Thank you, Lord,
that you are here with me,
and that your love surrounds me.

SALLY ANN WRIGHT

8 Lord, when we sin,
and we know it and are sorry,
and we ask you to forgive us,
please hear our prayer.
Listen from heaven,
and forgive us.

SOLOMON, BASED ON 1 KINGS 8:46-50

9
Lord, teach me to pray
with quiet words, and spaces
to hear what you have to say.

SUE DOGGETT

## 10

Open my eyes so I can see
all of the good things you give to me.
Shine light on my path,
make it bright for me,
Holy Trinity.

MARION THOMAS

## 11

Open my ears and let me hear you.
Open my eyes and let me see you.
Open my heart and let me love you,
Great God in heaven.

JONATHAN WILLIAMS

## 12

Sometimes when I come to pray
my thoughts wander, Lord,
and I think about other things.
Please help me to pray.

KIERAN, AGED 8

### 13

Speak, Lord, in the stillness,
While I wait for you,
Hush my heart to listen
In expectancy.

EMILY MAY GRIMES CRAWFORD

### 14 Speak, Lord,
because I am listening.

BASED ON 1 SAMUEL 3:9

### 15

Lord, you do not speak in a loud voice like thunder
but a small, quiet voice.
Help me listen to you and to hear
that small, quiet voice.

BASED ON 1 KINGS 19:12

### 16

Lord, do not leave us or forget us.
Help us to do the good things
you want us to do.

SOLOMON, BASED ON 1 KINGS 8:57–58

17

Lord, may everyone,
wherever they live on earth,
know that you are God
and there is no other.

SOLOMON, BASED ON 1 KINGS 8:60

18 Help me to seek you with all my heart
and trust you with all that I am.

BETHAN JAMES

19 Father in heaven,
may the thought of you
not make me feel like a frightened bird
but like a child waking up from sleep
to see the face of someone he loves.

BASED ON A PRAYER BY SØREN KIERKEGAARD

20 God the Father, my hope,
God the Son, my refuge,
God, the Holy Spirit, my protection,
Glory to thee, Holy Trinity.

FROM THE EASTERN ORTHODOX TRADITION

21 As tall trees reach for light,
and the waves come rushing to the shore
let me want to come to you, Lord.

SALLY ANN WRIGHT

22

Thank you that you know my name
and you care about me.

POPPY, AGED 5

## 23

From the sun's rising
To the sun's setting,
I want to praise you,
Lord!

BASED ON PSALM 113:3

## 24

Come and sing for joy to God;
let us come before him and say thank you!
For God is great!
He holds in his hands the foundations of the earth,
the mountain tops and the depths of the sea.
Come, bow down and worship him.
Kneel before the Lord, the Creator.
For he is our God, and we are his people.
He loves us and takes care of us.

BASED ON PSALM 95

## 25

You are awesome, Lord!
When I look at all the stars in the sky
I think how amazing you are!

OLIVER, AGED 8

## 26

Holy, holy, holy, Lord God almighty,
You are worthy, Lord God,
To receive praise and glory, honour and blessing.

BASED ON A PRAYER BY ST FRANCIS OF ASSISI

## 27

Praise God, from whom all blessings flow;
Praise him, all creatures here below;
Praise him above, you heavenly host;
Praise Father, Son, and Holy Ghost.

BISHOP THOMAS KEN

## 28

I'll praise you, God,
and I'll worship you
because you are so wonderful,
and you made the whole wide world!
You're great and good,
marvellous and mighty,
ever loving, everlasting,
everywhere.

JAN GODFREY

## 29

Let everyone know
that you alone are God!
Let them praise you!
For you are great and do wonderful things.
Teach me your ways, Lord,
so that my life will be good
and I will do nothing to hurt anyone else.

BASED ON PSALM 86:9–11

## 30

The birds praise you,
The bees praise you,
And I want to praise you, too!

IWONA, AGED 6

## 31

Thank you, Lord, you are great and good
and your love lasts for ever.
I will praise you now and for ever!

BASED ON 1 CHRONICLES 16:34–36

## 32

Let us praise and glorify God for ever.
Let heaven and earth praise your glory:
All creatures in heaven,
On earth and under the earth,
The sea and everything in it.
Let us praise and glorify God for ever.

BASED ON A PRAYER BY ST FRANCIS OF ASSISI

**33**

Shout for joy!
Everyone tell God how great he is!
Everything you do is awesome, Lord.
You have done great things!

BASED ON PSALM 66:1–3

**34** God who made the universe,
God who made the world and everything in it,
Thank you for letting me live in it.

GARETH, AGED 8

**35** Butterflies thank you for wings to fly,
fish give thanks for the sea.
Birds give thanks with the songs they sing,
but I thank you for making me me!

BETHAN JAMES

36  God, you are great!
You are wise and powerful.
You know things that no one else can know
and you have shown secret things to me.
You have given me wisdom
and helped me when I needed it most.
Thank you, God.

BASED ON DANIEL 2:20–23

37  There is no one like you, Lord,
and you are my God.

BASED ON 1 CHRONICLES 17:20

38 Shout for joy to the Lord, all the earth.
Worship him with gladness,
and come before him with joyful songs.
Know that the Lord is God.
It is he who made us;
we are his people and we belong to him.
Give thanks to God and praise him,
for the Lord is good;
he will always love us
and he never lets us down.

BASED ON PSALM 100

39
Give me a voice to praise you, Lord,
and a heart to love you.

MARION THOMAS

**40**

Lord, you are wise and wonderful.
You know when the mountain goats give birth,
and watch over the deer with her fawn.
You give speed to the ostrich
and strength to the horse.
You make hawks fly high and eagles soar.
Lord, you are wise and wonderful.

BASED ON JOB 39

**41**

Dear God,
you have given me all that I have.
Help me to love you with all my heart.

LIZZIE, AGED 7

**42**

As eagles love the wind,
As dolphins love the water,
As cats love a cosy corner,
Let me love you, Lord.

SALLY ANN WRIGHT

## 43

Lord, you are my shepherd.
Thank you for giving me everything I need.

BASED ON PSALM 23:1

## 44 Thank you,
God, that you are always there.
It makes me feel better.

JON, AGED 6

## 45

Thank you, God, for being there in the silence.
Thank you for being there in the dark.
Thank you for giving me peace.

MARION THOMAS

## 46

Lord, you made me just as I am.
Thank you for giving me life,
for loving me and taking care of me.

BASED ON JOB 10:8,12

47 Lord, you are kind and loving,
and you are slow to get cross.
You do not punish me for the terrible things I do,
because you love me so much.
You not only forgive me,
but you forget that I have done something wrong.
You are kinder than the best parent in the world,
and you have promised always to look after me.

BASED ON PSALM 103:8–14

48 Thank you for good things, Lord,
bread on the table
and love in our lives.

BASED ON 1 CHRONICLES 29:11, 14

49 Lord, be merciful to us and bless us,
and may your face always smile on us.
Let the whole world sing for joy,
because you are wise and good.
May everyone praise you, O God,
may everyone on earth praise you.
Then you will give us all we need
and you will richly bless us.

BASED ON PSALM 67

50 You are so good to me,
Lord.
I have so much to
say thank you for!

JULIET, AGED 7

51 Lord God, you are worthy
to receive glory, honour and power,
for you created all things,
and by your will all things in creation
were given life.

BASED ON REVELATION 4:11

52 God, you can do anything.
    Nothing is too hard for you.
    You can do more than I can even imagine.
    Help me not to be too afraid to ask.

BASED ON EPHESIANS 3:20

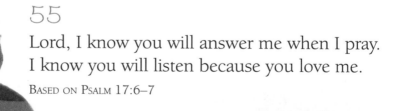

53 Please help me, Lord,
    when things are hard for me
    and I am tempted to give up.

BETHAN JAMES

54

Are you busy, Lord?
You must have so many people wanting to talk to you.
Will you have time to listen to me now?

ALEX, AGED 7

55

Lord, I know you will answer me when I pray.
I know you will listen because you love me.

BASED ON PSALM 17:6–7

56 O God, you are my hope and strength,
   always there in times of trouble.
   Therefore I will not be afraid,
   even though things are difficult for me.

BASED ON PSALM 46

## 57

You are a God who is always kind,
slow to get angry and always gentle and loving.
Be kind to me now, Lord,
be gentle and loving to me now,
because I need your help.
I need you to comfort me.

BASED ON PSALM 86:15–17

## 58

Thank you for being there, God,
when I wake up in the morning.
Thank you for being there,
when I go to sleep at night.

LAURA, AGED 6

59
Lord, there is no one like you
in heaven above or earth below.
You promised to love us and you do love us.
You have always kept your promises.

BASED ON 1 KINGS 8:23–24

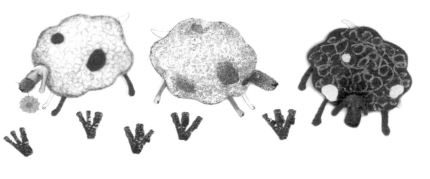

60 I do like sheep, God.
I like their woolly bodies.
I like their friendly faces.
I like the way they 'baa'
and laugh and run away.
Help me to remember
that you are like a good shepherd
who looks after me.

JAN GODFREY

### 61

You know what I was like today, Lord.
I was angry
I was selfish
I was greedy
I was proud
I was unkind
I was unhelpful.
Please forgive me.

JONATHAN WILLIAMS

### 62

Lord, you love me so much!
You even knew my name
before I was born,
before my mum and dad did!
But in case you forget,
as there are so many people in the
world,
I'll whisper it now...

JAN GODFREY

## 63

You're my real friend, God.
Sometimes I get upset
because people call me by my sister's name.
But you know my name,
my birthday and all about me.

HELEN, AGED 7

## 64

Lord, I can have no secrets from you.
Lord, I don't need to hide things from you.
You know everything and you can forgive everything.
Teach me to be sorry so that you can forgive me.

SALLY ANN WRIGHT

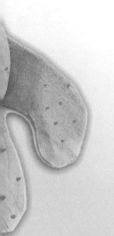

## 65

Lord God, you know when I am cross or grumpy
and when I am kind to other people.
Thank you that you know all about me
and you still love me.

BETHAN JAMES

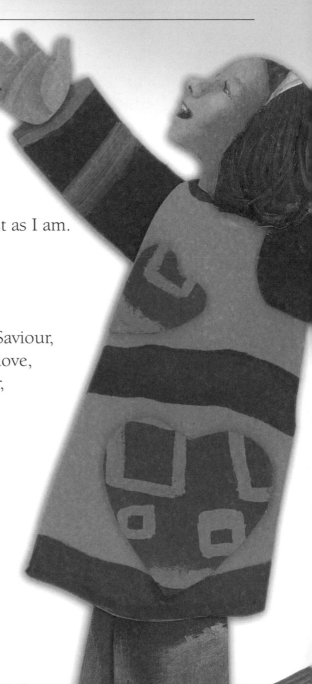

66

Thank you, Father God,
that you made me
and that I am special to you.
Thank you for loving me, just as I am.

SALLY ANN WRIGHT

67

May the grace of Christ our Saviour,
And the Father's boundless love,
With the Holy Spirit's favour,
Rest upon us from above.

JOHN NEWTON

68

You love me, God!
You care about me
and you give me all I need.

ANDREW, AGED 6

## 69

I love you Lord, because you heard me
when I asked for help.
You listened when I needed you,
because you love me.

BASED ON PSALM 116:1–6

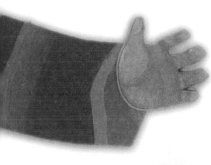

## 70

You make me feel special, Lord,
not because of anything I have done,
or because of what I haven't done,
or because of what I might do in the future,
but just because you love me.

MARION THOMAS

71

Thank you, God,
for my family and friends,
who love me and care for me
today and every day.

BETHAN JAMES

72

O God,
you know how busy
I must be this day.
If I forget you,
please don't forget me.

TRADITIONAL

73

O Lord,
help me to love you
with all my heart.

BRONWYN, AGED 4

74 Jesus, friend of little children,
    be a friend to me;
    take my hand, and ever keep me
    close to thee.

WALTER J. MATHAM

75

Lord God, you made me, you love me,
you gave me family and friends.
Teach me how to love you, too,
and to be kind to the people around me.

MARION THOMAS

76 Thank you, Father God, for blessing me
    With things to do and time to rest,
    For food to eat, for toys, for friends,
    For people who care about me and look after me.
    Thank you, Father God.

RHONA DAVIES

77 Bless our home, dear Lord.
Teach us to love one another,
support and help one another,
and forgive one another,
as you forgive us.

SALLY ANN WRIGHT

78 Lord Jesus,
you were part of the great family on earth,
and all over the world there are families big and small;
mums and dads, girls and boys,
dozens and dozens of faraway cousins.
Families are fun!
Sometimes they're quiet and sometimes they're noisy;
sometimes they're sad and sometimes they're happy,
sometimes with special meals together.
They squabble and quarrel and make it all up again.
Thank you for your great family
of all the people in the world.

JAN GODFREY

79

Bless our home, Father God, so that
we are grateful for food while it is here to eat,
and learn about each other
while they are here to love.

JONATHAN WILLIAMS

80

Thank you, dear God, for my parents
who love me and take care of me.
Help me to be good,
to listen to them and learn from them,
and to love them as much as they love me.

BETHAN JAMES

81

Lord, bless my home.
Help us to help each other.
Help us to be kind to anyone
who comes to us for help.

RHONA DAVIES

## 82

Please God,
look after everyone in my family.
Whether at home or far away,
keep them safe and well today.

BETHAN JAMES

## 83

I love my family, Lord.
I love it when we can all be together
and do fun things!

CARRIE, AGED 7

## 84

Lord, I am so lucky to have people
who love me and take care of me.
If I lost all of my special things
it would be very sad;
but if I lost my family,
nothing and no one could replace them.
Help me to show that I love them today.

MARION THOMAS

85 God in heaven, hear my prayer,
keep me in thy loving care.
Be my guide in all I do,
and please bless those who love me too.

TRADITIONAL

86

Thank you, Lord,
for my family, for food to eat
and a warm bed to sleep in at night.

KATHARINA, AGED 6

87

My big brother doesn't
believe in you, God.
Thank you that you
believe in him.

ANGELA, AGED 7

88 Teach me, Lord,
to work at everything I do
as if I am doing it for you.
Help me, Lord,
to be kind to people around me
as if I am being kind to you.

BASED ON MATTHEW 25:40

89

Dear God, help me to share my toys.
Sometimes I don't want to share
and we have arguments.
I'm sorry I got cross with my friend today.

CHRISTINE WRIGHT

90
Sometimes it's great being with my friends.
But sometimes we argue and get cross with each other.
I'm sorry when we spoil the fun
by being selfish or unkind.

JACK, AGED 8

91 Thank you, Lord, for my friends,
and for all the fun we have together.
Please help me
to be a good friend to them.

BETHAN JAMES

92 Lord Jesus, Good Shepherd,
You look after me and care for me.
Lord Jesus, Good Shepherd,
Look after my family, friends and pets today.

BETHAN JAMES

93

Thank you, God, for our animals.
We love our cats and dogs and rabbits.
They're real friends to look after
and to stroke and to talk to.
They know our voices
and they seem to understand
and listen when we're feeling sad.
They're fun and bouncy
and play with us when we're happy.
Help us to take care of our pets
and to help look after the animals in our world.

JAN GODFREY

## 94

Please look after my hamsters,
Cookie and Ellie.
When Sherbert dies,
please look after her too.

MELEK-MARY, AGE 5

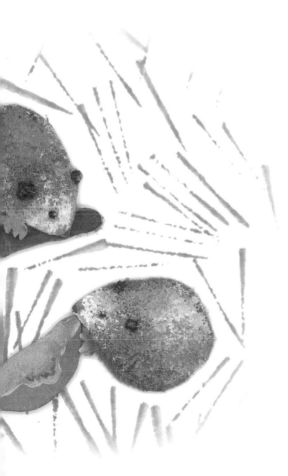

## 95

For woods and fields,
For sea and sky,
For flowers, trees,
Family and friends,
All the creatures around me,
And all your gifts,
Thank you, God!

SALLY ANN WRIGHT

## 96

I come to you, Father God,
to thank you for all you have given me,
to say sorry for all the wrong things I have said or done,
and to pray for other people who need your help.

MARION THOMAS

## 97

I am sorry, Lord,
because today…
I didn't listen
I didn't see
I didn't speak kindly
I didn't help
I didn't make peace
I didn't forgive
I didn't love
I am sorry, Lord.

JONATHAN WILLIAMS

98

You know everything I think, Lord.
You know that I have come to say sorry now.

ROSIE, AGED 6

99

Help me to pray, Lord.
Help me to mean the words I say.
Help me to be sorry when I say sorry.
Help me to say thank you
and mean thank you.
Help me, please, to pray, Lord.

SALLY ANN WRIGHT

100

Be kind to me, Lord, as you have promised.
Be generous and forgive me,
Because I know I have done a terrible thing.
I am ashamed and so very sorry.
Please, God, help me to start all over again.

DAVID, BASED ON PSALM 51:1–12

## 101

Sometimes I make mistakes
and sometimes I can't help being horrible.
But sometimes I am nasty
  because I am really angry with someone
  and they have hurt me.
  Please forgive me, Lord.

HANNAH ROSE, AGED 8

## 102

I am sorry, Lord,
because today…
I complained
I argued
I moaned
I sulked
I gossiped
I am sorry, Lord.

JONATHAN WILLIAMS

## 103

Help me to stop telling lies, Lord.
Help me to stop getting angry.
Help me to say sorry before night-time.

BASED ON EPHESIANS 4:25–26

## 104

Dear God, I'm really sorry that I often do wrong things.
Sometimes I'm cross and grumpy.
Sometimes I'm naughty and disobedient.
Sometimes I'm horrid and hurtful.
Sometimes I'm selfish and want my own way.
Sometimes I stamp and SHOUT!
Sometimes I tell little fibs
and pretend they don't matter.
Sometimes I make other people sad,
and that makes you sad, too.
Please forgive me
and help me to say sorry to other people too
and I'll try to do the right things next time.

JAN GODFREY

**105**

Lord, hear my prayer.
Listen from heaven,
the place where you live,
and when you hear, please forgive.

SOLOMON, BASED ON 1 KINGS 8:30

**106** I am so, so sorry, Lord.
I hurt someone else,
and I know that means I hurt you, too.

SALLY ANN WRIGHT

**107**

Please, Lord,
forgive me for all the bad things I have thought
in the past;
forgive me for all the bad things I have said
in the past;
forgive me for all the bad things I have done
in the past;
and forgive me for all the bad things
I thought and said and did today.

BETHAN JAMES

108

Dear God,
I am sorry for all the things
I have done today to make you sad.

OWEN, AGED 5

109

Forgive me, Lord,
because today…
I wasn't kind
I wasn't patient
I wasn't gentle
I wasn't thoughtful
I wasn't friendly
I wasn't generous
I wasn't loving
Forgive me, Lord.

JONATHAN WILLIAMS

110 Lord, you promise to forgive me
as long as I can forgive others.
Help me to forgive today.

BASED ON MARK 11:25

111

I am sorry, Lord,
because my friend was not nice to me today,
and I can still remember when she was horrible last week.

ANNIE, AGED 7

## 112

Lord,
help me to forgive other people
when they hurt me,
just as you forgive me.

BASED ON EPHESIANS 4:2

## 113

Father God,
someone was really unkind to me today.
Help me to remember the times when I have been unkind,
and when I needed forgiveness,
so that I can learn to forgive them.

BETHAN JAMES

## 114 When people are difficult or selfish,
help me to forgive them.

BASED ON A PRAYER BY MOTHER TERESA

## 115

The good I do today will soon be forgotten.
Help me to do good anyway.
Help me, Lord, to give the best I have, whatever happens,
because what matters most is doing my best for you.

Based on a prayer by Mother Teresa

## 116

Please help me to
say sorry.

Alice, aged 5

## 117

Please help me to learn to do the right thing;
help me to be honest and fair.

BASED ON PSALM 101:2

## 118

Lord, help me to know you better,
so I can love you,
and help me to love you,
so I can do the things you want me to do
willingly and without complaining.

BASED ON A PRAYER BY ST AUGUSTINE

## 119

I want to be generous, Lord,
but often I am mean.
I want to be kind, Lord,
but often I am not.
I want to say the right thing,
but often the wrong thing comes out.
I need your help, Lord. Please help me.

BASED ON ROMANS 7:19

120 Lord,
   I have been grumpy,
   and done things
   I was told not to do.
   I am sorry.

   OLIVER, AGED 6

121 Show me how to live, Lord,
   teach me the right way.
   Guide me and teach me
   for you are my God.
   Forget my sins;
   remember only that you love me.

   BASED ON PSALM 25:4–6

122 When people tell me I am being kind for the wrong
   reasons, help me to be kind anyway.

   BASED ON A PRAYER BY MOTHER TERESA

123 I am sorry, Lord.
   I forgot to say thank you, and I wasn't kind to my friends.

   SOPHIE, AGED 6

124 On breezy, blustering, gusty days;
In the wild, windy night,
Thank you for your Holy Spirit
Who shows me wrong from right.

BASED ON JOHN 3:8

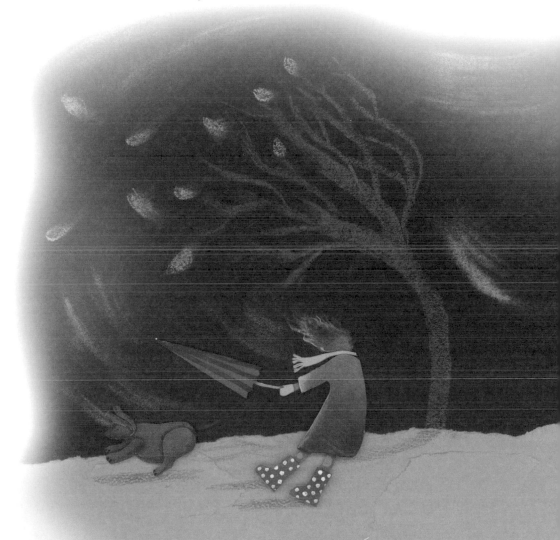

## 125

Lord God,
I'm young and I know nothing.
Help me know good from bad,
give me wisdom to know
what you want me to do,
and a heart to love you always.

SOLOMON, BASED ON 1 KINGS 3:7, 9

## 126

Here I am, Lord, it's me.
Talk to me and help me to listen,
and show me what you want me to do.

IZZIE, AGED 7

127 Father God, I need guidance.
I don't know the way
and I am not sure where to go.
Please God, help me.
Watch over each step I take
and guide me in the right path.

BASED ON A PRAYER BY ST AUGUSTINE

128

Teach me, Lord, to seek you,
Help me, Lord, to find you,
Let me learn to love you.

BASED ON A PRAYER BY ST ANSELM

129

Lord, when I am cross and want to be unkind,
when I am jealous and want to be unfair,
when I am tired and I don't want to listen,
help me to think how I would feel
if someone was unkind or unfair or uncaring to me,
and help me to be kind.

JONATHAN WILLIAMS

## 130

Lord, please be
a bright flame before me,
a guiding star above me,
a smooth path beneath me,
and a good shepherd behind me,
today and every day.

BASED ON A PRAYER BY ST COLUMBA

## 131

Lord, please give me
the peace to accept what cannot be changed,
the courage to change what must be altered,
and the wisdom to know the difference.

BASED ON A PRAYER BY REINHOLD NIEBUHR

132 Lord, your word is a lamp
   shining on my life
   and teaching me the right way to live.

BASED ON PSALM 119:105

133

What should I do, Lord?
I really don't know.
Please help me to know it,
and then when I know,
help me to do it.

MARIA, AGED 8

134

Thank you, Father God,
that you know what I need
before I do.
Help me to take one step
at a time and to trust you
to give me the strength
for hard times just when I need it.

BETHAN JAMES

135 Be kind to me, Lord, and make me happy.
You are so good, so ready to forgive,
and you always have enough love
for anyone who comes and asks for your help.

BASED ON PSALM 86:3–5

136

Help me to be happy when others are happy.
Help me not to be jealous.
Help me to be pleased if they have nice things.
Help me not to be envious—
because sometimes it's hard.

BASED ON 1 CORINTHIANS 13

137

Father God, I have so much
and some people have so little.
Thank you for all that I have.
But help me to know that things
will never make me happy.
Only you can do that.

MARION THOMAS

## 138

I know you are there,
Lord Jesus,
in happy times,
when I'm smiling,
having fun.
Well, I'm happy now,
so please be here
with me today!

CHRISTINE WRIGHT

## 139

Lord, I am happy!
All my friends like me!
Everything is great!

REBECCA, AGED 6

## 140

I am praying to you, Lord.
Please answer me.
Please answer me because you love me.
Please help me because I am in trouble.

BASED ON PSALM 69:13, 16–17

## 141

Lord, you promise to hear when we pray.
Listen to me now.
Please help me with the hard things I have to do.
Please make me brave.

DYLAN, AGED 9

## 142

Lord, you alone are God.
You have made heaven and earth.
Now please help me,
so that everyone will know
that you alone are God.

KING HEZEKIAH, BASED ON 2 KINGS 19:15, 19

## 143

Listen to my prayer, Lord;
I need you to hear me.
I ask for your help whenever I'm in trouble,
and I know you will answer me.
No one else can do what you can do!

BASED ON PSALM 86:6–8

## 144

Lord, you are the living God.
You rescue and save us.
You perform great miracles!

BASED ON DANIEL 6:26–27

## 145

I don't care what anyone else says.
You are real, Lord,
and you helped me when I needed you.
I will worship you, and I will thank you,
because you answered
when I asked for help.

FROM JONAH 2:9

## 146

I need you, Lord.
Please come close to me,
help me, rescue me,
protect me.

BASED ON PSALM 69:18

14·7 Sometimes everything changes,
and I wish it would stay the same.
There are new houses and new schools,
new friends and new teachers,
new neighbours and new streets,
new places and new faces.
Sometimes it's a little bit scary,
but sometimes it's FUN!
And I know you're with me, God,
however I grow and wherever I go,
and you are always the same,
yesterday, today and for ever.

JAN GODFREY

14·8 Lord, be with me
because it is dark and I am afraid.

KIERAN, AGED 6

14·9

Do not be far from me, Lord,
For trouble is near
And there is no one to help.

BASED ON PSALM 22:11

## 150

Loving Father, please look after me.
I am not well.
I hurt a lot.
Please make me better.

Jenni, aged 6

## 151

Come close to me, Lord,
because without you I cannot be strong.
Come quickly to help me.

Based on Psalm 22:19

## 152

Lord, look down on me and be kind
because I am ill.
Help me to bear it patiently.

Based on a prayer by St Francis of Assisi

## 153

Lord, I need help.
Who can help me but you?
My help comes from you,
the God who made heaven and earth!
You will always take care of me.
You promise that you will watch over me,
day and night, wherever I am
and whatever I am doing.
Thank you!

Based on Psalm 121

## 154

Lord, please give me a healthy body,
a curious mind and a kind and generous nature.

Marion Thomas

## 155

Lord, I am not good enough to receive you,
but just say the word
and I know I can be healed.

Based on Matthew 8:8

## 156

I am sorry, God, that I was unkind
and said things that made someone sad.

BETHAN JAMES

## 157

Lord Jesus,
sometimes in my family
people are angry;
sometimes they are sad.
Please help us.

RHONA DAVIES

## 158

When everything is dark
and I feel weak and sad,
help me to know that you are there, Lord.

BASED ON A PRAYER BY ST IGNATIUS OF LOYOLA

159 Lord, you know when I am sad
and when I am lonely.
Lord, I am sad and lonely now.
Please be my friend.

ROBERT, AGED 7

160

Lord, I feel so sad I can hardly eat.
I am like a little lost owl.
I feel so lonely that I cannot sleep,
and I can't stop crying.
Lord, hear my prayer!
Please come close and help me.

BASED ON PSALM 102

161

Be near me, Lord,
in the dark moments of my life.
Help me when I feel so sad
that I cannot remember
what it feels like to be happy.

SALLY ANN WRIGHT

## 162

Lord, hear my prayer!
Don't turn away from me
because I need you.
Bend down to listen to me,
and answer me quickly when I call to you.

BASED ON PSALM 102:1

163 Help me to know that you love me, Lord.
And help me, Lord, to trust you,
so that nothing can frighten me or worry me.

BASED ON A PRAYER BY ST IGNATIUS OF LOYOLA

164 When I feel alone,
help me to remember
that you are here with me.

VICTORIA, AGED 7

165

Turn to me and be kind, Lord,
for I am lonely and sad.

BASED ON PSALM 25:16

166

I am afraid, Lord.
I feel very alone.
Please stay with me.

ASHWIN, AGED 5

## 167

Lord Jesus,
you told us not be worried about anything,
but I am worried about tomorrow.
Help me to tell you about my worries
and then to trust you to help me.

BASED ON MATTHEW 6:34

## 168

Lord, you are love and you are wisdom.
You are rest and you are peace.
You are my protector and my defender,
you are courage and you are hope.
You are eternal life,
great and wonderful Lord.

BASED ON A PRAYER BY ST FRANCIS OF ASSISI

169 Come close to me, Lord, and hear my prayer.
Answer me, because I need your help.
Look after me, because I love you.
Help me, because I trust you and you are my God.

BASED ON PSALM 86:1–2

170

Thank you, Jesus,
for loving me so much.
Help me to know that I am your friend.

ALEX, AGED 7

171

I was in deep, deep trouble, Lord,
but I prayed to you, and you answered me.
I cried out, 'Help!' and you heard my cry.
I thought nothing could save me,
but you heard my prayer,
you heard my cry for help,
and you saved me.

BASED ON JONAH 2:2, 7

## 172

I don't want to say goodbye, Lord.
I am not ready.
I don't want things to change, Lord.
I am not ready.
Help me to be happy with what is past,
make me brave to face today,
and give me faith to face the future.

JONATHAN WILLIAMS

## 173

Lord, someone
I love has died
and I am so,
so unhappy.

DANIEL, AGED 7

174 Lord Jesus,
   you said there are
   many rooms in God's house.
   Please make a special room
   ready for me,
   and all the people in my family
   and all those I love,
   when it is our turn to die.

BASED ON JOHN 14:2

175

Lord Jesus, when somebody we love has died we're very sad.
But we know we'll say 'hello!' again one day,
with new and special bodies in a new and sparkling world.
Help us to remember all the happy times,
the cosy-cuddly times,
the eating-together times,
the looking-at-books-together times,
the watching-TV-together times,
the round-the-kitchen-table-chatting times,
the 'look-at-me-on-the-swing' times.
Help us to remember voices and faces,
and all that we shared, because all these things
are part of your great love that lasts for ever and ever.

JAN GODFREY

## 176

Sometimes it is hard
to love people, Lord.
Show me how
to start with small things.
Help me to give a small gift first.
Help me to smile at them.

BASED ON A PRAYER BY MOTHER TERESA

## 177

Lord Jesus,
you made blind people see.
Help me to see you
in the people around me
and be kind to them.

SALLY ANN WRIGHT

## 178

Help me, Lord, to live today
knowing you are there to help me.

JOSH, AGED 6

## 179

Dear God, sometimes I point at other people
and say they're not good at games
or clever at their work.
Sometimes I think they don't wear cool clothes
or have the right toys or the latest games,
or they're just different from me.
Help me to see that these things don't matter
and to like other people for who they are
and not for what they have or what they can do.

JAN GODFREY

## 180

Make my heart like yours, Lord.
Help me to love you.
Help me to love those around me.
Help me to love even my enemies.

JONATHAN WILLIAMS

181 O God,
Help me never to judge another person
until I have walked two weeks in his moccasins.

BASED ON A SIOUX PRAYER

182 Lord, please give me
hands that are quick to give and slow to take,
feet that go where you want me to be,
eyes that see the best in everyone,
ears that hear only good things,
a voice that speaks the truth kindly,
and a loving, forgiving heart.

SALLY ANN WRIGHT

## 183

Lord, let me not judge others
by what I see or hear,
without knowing
or understanding
anything about them.

BASED ON A PRAYER BY THOMAS À KEMPIS

## 184

Dear God, sometimes I am nasty about people
who have done something wrong.
Help me to remember that it's for you,
not me, to decide what's right and wrong,
and to see that I do wrong things myself.

JAN GODFREY

## 185

I heard bad things about someone yesterday, God,
and I told my friend, and he told someone else
and then everyone knew
and people were nasty to the boy,
and then I found it wasn't even true.
I wish I hadn't said anything.

DAVID, AGED 9

## 186

Give me hands to help others, Lord,
and feet to walk where you take me.

BASED ON A PRAYER BY MOTHER TERESA

## 187

Lord,
help me to be kind to the people I meet today.
Help me to be ready to be there
for anyone who needs my help.

RHONA DAVIES

## 188

I have been kind to Emily,
Kaysha and Neida this week.
Please help me to be kind to Liam.
He's a boy and it's harder.

MELEK-MARY, AGE 5

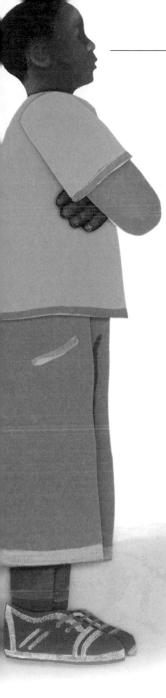

189

Lord Jesus,
you helped lame people walk.
Help me to walk
where you want me to go.

SALLY ANN WRIGHT

190

Help me, Lord, to do the things I should,
To be kind to others, thoughtful, good;
Help me as I work and play,
To love, as you do, every day.

REBECCA WESTON

191

Help me to love other people.
Help me to care when people suffer
from the cruelty of others.
Help me to speak out
for those who cannot speak for themselves.

JONATHAN WILLIAMS

192 For all the children of the world,
let there be love,
peace and happiness.

GRACE, AGED 7

193
Lord,
you have given me
so many good things.
Sometimes I forget
how lucky I am.
Help me to remember,
and to share
with other people.

MARION THOMAS

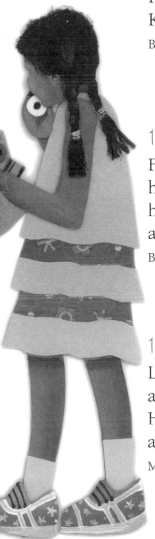

## 194

Thank you, Father God, for a new day.
Help me to be kind to all the people I meet.
Keep me from cross words and from being selfish.

BETHAN JAMES

## 195

Father God,
help me not to want more things than I need,
help me not to judge other people by what they have,
and help me to share everything you have given me.

BASED ON MATTHEW 6:19–20

## 196

Lord, you gave food to people who were hungry
and you cared about them.
Help me to share what I have with those who need it,
and to care about other people too.

MARION THOMAS

### 197

May everything I say,
and everything I think,
be kind and good.
O Lord,
my rock and my protector.

BASED ON PSALM 19:14

### 198

Lord Jesus,
the wind and the waves obeyed you.
Help me to obey you, too.

SALLY ANN WRIGHT

### 199

Dear God, there's no school today.
Mum wants me to help tidy my room
and I want to play on my new X-box.
What should I do?

CHARLIE, AGED 7

200 Give me the light to find my way when shadows fall.
Be my steady guiding star, Father God of all.

A PRAYER FROM ISRAEL

201

Help me, God, in everything I do.
Show me how to do what is right and good.

BETHAN JAMES

**202** God, you made the world
and I love living in it!

ELENA, AGED 5

**203**

Creator God, you made the world!
Tall trees and tiny flowers,
silver fish and flying insects,
birds and beasts, speckled, dappled,
spotted, striped and patterned.
Creator God, you made the world
and it is very good!

RHONA DAVIES

**205**

Thank you, God,
for birds that fly
and creatures wild
and for making me,
a little child.

BETHAN JAMES

**204**

Dear Father, hear and bless
Beasts and singing birds,
And guard with tenderness
Small things that have no words.

TRADITIONAL

206 You have done so many great things, Lord!
The world is full of the creatures you have made.
The oceans are huge, and full of every kind of living being.
All creatures trust you to give them food,
and you satisfy us all with good things.

BASED ON PSALM 104:24–28

207 Thank you, God, for the cool rain
which makes things grow.
Thank you for noisy thunderstorms
when I am safe inside.

ELLA, AGED 8

208

For springtime breezes and summer sun,
Thank you, Lord.
For autumn winds and winter snows,
Thank you, Lord, thank you, Lord.

SALLY ANN WRIGHT

## 209

Thank you, God, for the world you have made.
Thank you for the warm shining sun,
And green grass and blossom,
And wind in the trees
And time to play outside till bedtime.

BETHAN JAMES

## 210

This is the day that the Lord has made,
let us rejoice and be glad in it.

BASED ON PSALM 118:23–24

## 211

Autumn…
Red leaves, yellow leaves,
orange leaves, brown leaves,
crunchy leaves, swirling leaves,
running-along-the-ground leaves,
deep leaves, piles of leaves,
let me jump in them, please!
God you made it, God you gave it.
Thank you for it, thank you for it.

MARION THOMAS

**212** Spotty ladybirds, stripy snails,
Tiny spiders, buzzing bees,
Slimy slugs with silvery trails,
Wiggly worms and centipedes,
Crawling creatures with long tails:
Thank you, God, you made all these.

BETHAN JAMES

**213**

Your world is awesome, God!
Everything you made is amazing.
And you, God, you are amazing!

ANTONIO, AGED 8

Thank you, God,
you made the tree,
the patterned bark,
214 the shiny leaves.
Thank you, God,
you made the flower,
the coloured petals,
leafy stem.
Thank you, God,
you made the bee,
gossamer wings,
and rhythmic buzz.
Thank you, God,
you made the bird,
soaring, singing,
fluttering, flying.
Thank you, God,
you made cat and dog,
mouse and frog,
and you made me.

SALLY ANN WRIGHT

215
Thank you, God,
for making giraffes tall,
and hamsters small,
and ladybirds crawl,
and creatures all
around us!

BETHAN JAMES

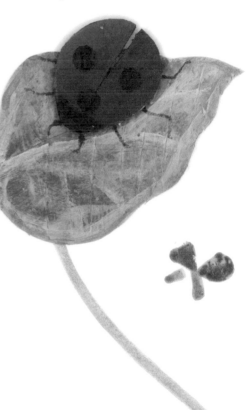

## 216

Thank you, God, for the wonder of snow.
It's so beautiful!
I love all the whirly flakes that drift like white stars.
I love the new, cold, sparkly world outside.
I love making snowmen with carrotty noses.
You've made each snowflake perfectly,
and each one is different.
For the wonder of snow, thank you, God.

JAN GODFREY

## 217

For sunshine, blue skies, fluffy clouds,
thank you, Creator God.
For dewdrops, raindrops, windy days,
thank you, Creator God.
For snowflakes, hoar frost, icicles,
thank you, Creator God.
For warm days, cold days,
wet days, dry days,
thank you, Creator God.

BETHAN JAMES

## 218

O Lord God, how great you are!
When I look at the sky,
and the moon and the stars,
I feel so tiny, I don't understand why you care about me.
O Lord God, how great you are!

BASED ON PSALM 8:1, 3–4

## 219

The sea is absolutely colourful today, God.
The sea is very straight.
So we are going to paddle!

MARTHA AND FLORA, AGED 2

## 220

Creator God, you made the world and it was very good.
Thank you for light and darkness,
rivers, streams and mountaintops,
sun, moon, stars and planets.
Creator God, you made the world and it is very good.
Thank you.

RHONA DAVIES

221 Lord, you have given me your world to care for;
   you have told me to look after
   everything you have created:
   the sheep and the cows, the dogs and the cats,
   and all the creatures that crawl on the earth;
   the birds in the sky, and the fish in the sea,
   the bees and butterflies, worms and caterpillars,
   and all the creatures that live in the waters.
   Lord, you have given me your world to care for;
   Thank you!

SALLY ANN WRIGHT

222

Thank you, God,
for eyes so I can see your world,
a mind so I can ask lots of questions
and a heart so I can love.

BETHAN JAMES

223 I want the world to be here when I grow up.
Help me to look after it now, God,
and not waste or spoil
all the good things you made.

ROSIE, AGED 8

224

Misty, moisty morning,
sunshine breaking through,
here's another day before me.
Lord God, I love you!

MARION THOMAS

## 225

Help your world, Father God.
People are suffering.
Some have lost their homes and families;
some people are starving;
others are in pain or dying.
Please comfort and help each one,
and help us to share our money,
our food, our love, our prayers,
to help them in their need.

RHONA DAVIES

## 226

I don't like watching the news, Lord,
because too many sad things are happening.
Thank you that I am safe
but please look after the people who are not safe
and who are afraid today.

MARK, AGED 9

227

I can't do anything to help, God,
but you can.
I'm asking you now to do something, please.

RYAN, AGED 7

229

Thank you, Lord Jesus,
that you are our hiding place
when bad things happen.

BASED ON PSALM 32:7

228

Watch, dear Lord,
with those who wake,
or watch, or weep tonight.
Let angels guard those who sleep.
Take care of those who are ill,
give rest to those who are weary,
help the dying,
and give hope to the suffering.

BASED ON A PRAYER BY ST AUGUSTINE

## 230

I had nothing when I was born,
and I shall take nothing with me when I die.
You have given me all that I have, Lord,
and it is yours to take away.

BASED ON JOB 1:21

## 231

Lord, please comfort people who
have no hope.
Protect those who are suffering.
Bring peace to your world.

SALLY ANN WRIGHT

## 232

Father God,
comfort and heal all those who suffer.
Give courage to those who are afraid.
Bring hope to those who have no hope
and give joy to those who are sad.

JONATHAN WILLIAMS

## 233

Lord, people are suffering.
Please give them your peace.

MATT, AGED 7

## 234

Creator God,
bring your light into all the dark places in this world.

MARION THOMAS

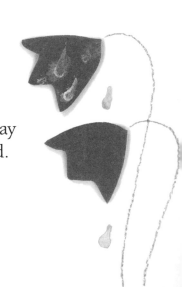

## 235

Father God,
people are fighting.
Please stop them hating each other.
Help them to be kind.

Emily, aged 6

## 236

I know people are dying all over the world
and you must be very busy, God.
But my brother has gone to be a soldier.
He's gone to dangerous places
a long way from home.
We miss him.
We worry about him
and all the other soldiers who are smiling today
and tomorrow might be hurt or dying or dead.
Look after my brother, God.
Please.

Ben Reynolds

### 237

Please, Lord,
bring peace and love and kindness
where there are wars
and fighting
and pain
and suffering
and hurting
and crying.

JONATHAN WILLIAMS

### 238

Where there is war, let there be peace.
Where there is hate, let there be love.
Where there is sadness, let there be joy.
Where there is suffering, let there be hope.

BASED ON A PRAYER BY ST IGNATIUS OF LOYOLA

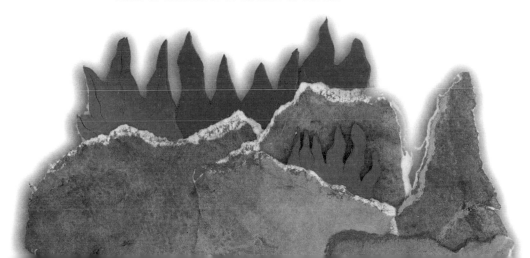

### 239

Help me to use good and helpful words
that please you, God,
not words that are rude or spiteful
or silly or unkind.

JAN GODFREY

### 240

Loving Father, you made everyone
and you love everyone!
Different ages and different sizes,
different shapes and different colours.
Help us to learn from one another,
share with one another,
and love one another.

BETHAN JAMES

## 241

Help me, Lord, to love my family.
Help my family to love the people they meet.
Help us all to love those in other countries.
Help all countries of the world
To love each other and live together in peace.
Lord, let it begin with me.

SALLY ANN WRIGHT

## 242

Thank you that you are our Father,
and we are your children.
Thank you that this makes us brothers and sisters.
But help us to love other people as if they are family,
and not quarrel with them as if they are family!

JAMIE, AGED 9

## 243

Thank you for my teachers.
Lord, I pray for children
who want to learn
but cannot go to school.

LUCY, AGED 6

## 244

Lord Jesus, you knew
what it was like to be very hungry.
You felt the pain of thirst.
Come now and help those who are suffering in your world,
and are hungry and thirsty.

JONATHAN WILLIAMS

245 Lord God,
there are many bad places in the world.
Please protect people who want to lead good lives,
and teach those who do wrong
the right way to live.

MARION THOMAS

246 Please stay with me, Lord,
so that your warm love
can touch other people
as you have touched me.

BASED ON A PRAYER BY MOTHER TERESA

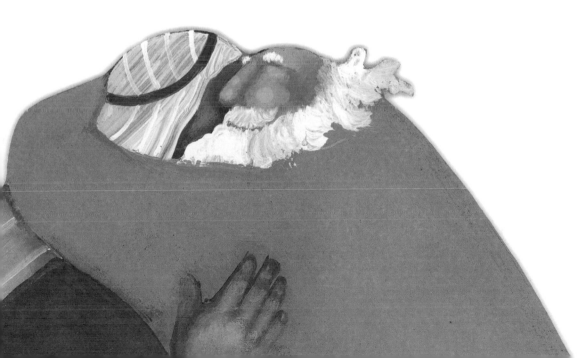

247

Open my eyes to see what the good Samaritan saw.
Make me wise to know what to do,
and make me willing to do what I can to help.

JONATHAN WILLIAMS

248

Help me, Lord,
to see the world as you see it,
to care for people in need as you care,
to love in the same way as you love.

BETHAN JAMES

249

Almighty God, Lord of the universe,
you are loving and caring,
you are strong and understanding.
Bless me now with all I need
to love and care for those around me,
to be strong to do only what is good,
and to be understanding if people are unkind to me.

A PRAYER FROM AUSTRALIA

250

I want to help, Lord.
Show me how.

MEGAN, AGED 8

251

Lord, you have
no eyes on earth but mine.
Help me to see
when people are in need
And to be willing
to help them.

BASED ON A PRAYER BY ST TERESA

## 252

Lord, when I am not well,
there are doctors and medicine
and people to take care of me.
Please look after children
in places where there is no doctor
and no one to help make them well.

MARION THOMAS

253 Lord, you have no body on earth but mine.
You have no hands but mine, no feet but mine.
Give me willing hands and feet
To go to people who are in need
And to do good things to help them.

BASED ON A PRAYER BY ST TERESA

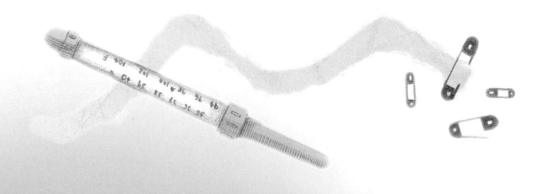

## 254

Father God, you have so much love to give.
Bless all those children in families
where there is no mother or father
and help them not to feel lonely or sad.

JOSEPH, AGED 8

## 255

Help us
to love each other,
to care for each other
and to be especially kind
to each other today.

SALLY ANN WRIGHT

## 256

Please look after people who are in hospital.
Help them when they feel afraid,
or alone,
or worried.
Help them when they are in pain.
Help the doctors and nurses
to look after them and make them well.

JONATHAN WILLIAMS

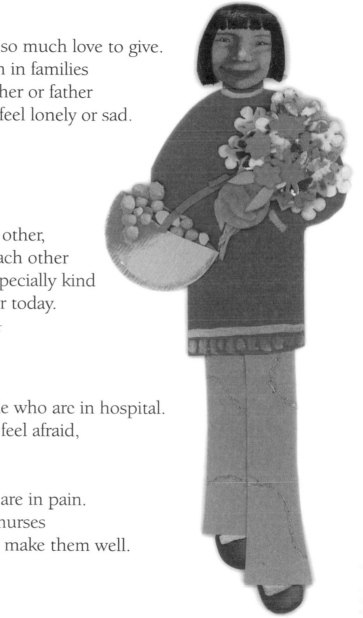

## 257

For what we are about to receive,
may the Lord make us truly thankful;
through Jesus Christ our Lord.

Traditional

## 258

The eagles give thanks for the mountains,
The fish give thanks for the sea,
We give thanks for our blessings
And for what we're about to receive.

A native American prayer

## 259

For every cup and plateful
Lord, make us truly grateful.

Traditional

260 We are hungry, Lord God,
and the food is hot,
so we just want to say thank you for it!

Harry, aged 7

261

To God who gives our daily bread
A thankful song we raise,
And pray that he who sends us food
May fill our hearts with praise.

Thomas Tallis

262 With your generous love, O God,
you have surrounded us with good things to enjoy.

SUE DOGGETT

263 Blessed are you,
Lord God of all creation,
for giving us all we need to eat today.

TRADITIONAL

**264** All good gifts around us
Are sent from heaven above.
Then thank the Lord, O thank the Lord,
For all his love.

MATTHIAS CLAUDIUS

**265**

Yours, Lord, is the greatness, the power,
the glory and the majesty,
for everything we have comes from you.

BASED ON 1 CHRONICLES 29:11–14

**266**

Heavenly Father, how I wish
that everybody had a dish
of rice or bread or meat each day
to help them grow and work and play.

JAN GODFREY

**267**

Thank you for all the good things
you give to us!

ALICE, AGED 5

## 268

God is great and God is good,
and we thank God for our food;
by God's hand we must be fed,
give us, Lord, our daily bread.

TRADITIONAL

## 269

Bless this food for our use,
and ourselves in your service,
Lord, we pray.

TRADITIONAL

## 270

For this and all his many mercies,
God's holy name be blessed and praised;
through Christ our Lord.

TRADITIONAL

## 271

Come, Lord Jesus, be our guest
and let this food, these gifts, be blessed.

A PRAYER FROM GERMANY

## 272

Thank you, Lord, for these gifts,
which you have freely given us.

TRADITIONAL

## 273

Lord, make me truly thankful for
these and all your blessings.

TRADITIONAL

## 274

May the Lord who feeds the little bird,
bless our food now, we pray.

A PRAYER FROM NORWAY

## 275

Thank you for the world so sweet,
Thank you for the food we eat,
Thank you for the birds that sing,
Thank you, God, for everything.

EDITH RUTTER LEATHAM

## 276

Lord, you are so great and good!
Thank you so much for this food.

LOTTIE, AGED 8

## 277

May we and all who share this food
have strength to live for you today.

TRADITIONAL

**278**

Our hands we fold,
our heads we bow,
for food and drink,
we thank you now.

TRADITIONAL

**279**

Each time we eat,
may we remember God's love to us.

A PRAYER FROM CHINA

**280**

God is great!
God is good!
Let us thank him
for our food.

TRADITIONAL

281 We thank you for the food before us,
we thank you for the family beside us,
and we thank you for the love between us.

ANON.

282 Thank you, Lord, for happy hearts,
for rain and sunny weather.
Thank you, Lord, for this good food,
and that we can be together.

TRADITIONAL

283 The bread is warm and fresh,
the water cool and clear.
Lord of all life, be with us,
Lord of all life, be near.

A PRAYER FROM NIGERIA

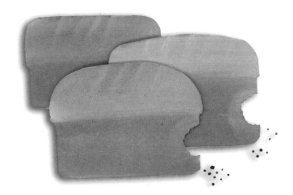

284
Good food, good meat,
good friends, let's eat!

TRADITIONAL

285 For food and drink and love outpoured,
thank you, thank you, thank you, Lord.

JAN GODFREY

286 For food that stays our hunger,
for rest that brings us ease,
for homes where memories linger,
we give our thanks for these.

TRADITIONAL

**287** It's Christmas!
I love Christmas Day best of all!

CHLOE, AGED 4

**288**
A long time ago,
Mary put her baby in a manger.
Thank you, God, that today we can know him.
A long time ago,
the angels sang because Jesus was born.
Thank you, God, that today we can worship him.
A long time ago,
shepherds hurried to see their Saviour.
Thank you, God, that today we can serve him.
A long time ago,
wise men brought Jesus gifts.
Thank you, God, that today we can love him.

SALLY ANN WRIGHT

**289**
With the angels and oxen,
the shepherds and stars,
with Mary and Joseph,
I thank you, Lord, for baby Jesus.

MARION THOMAS

290 May the joy of the angels,
the wonder of the shepherds,
and the peace of Jesus Christ,
fill our hearts this Christmas time.

TRADITIONAL

291

Dear Father God,
thank you for Christmas.
Thank you for the gift of Jesus
to be our friend, our Saviour and our king.

BETHAN JAMES

### 292

At the first Christmas, angels sang
announcing joy and peace on earth
because of Jesus, the Saviour's birth.
Now it's Christmas-time again,
and church bells ring, and people sing
glory to you, Lord, our newborn king!

JONATHAN WILLIAMS

### 293

Dear Father God,
Thank you for the message of peace
that Christmas brings to our world.

RHONA DAVIES

### 294
Lord Jesus,
it's Christmas!
It's your birthday!
What present
can I bring to you?

JACK, AGED 5

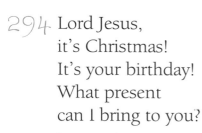

## 295

Lord, you were a tiny baby
in a manger, in Bethlehem.
You grew up to be a man
who helped people who were ill,
or sad, or lonely,
and you showed us how to love
other people as God does.
Thank you, Lord Jesus.

SALLY ANN WRIGHT

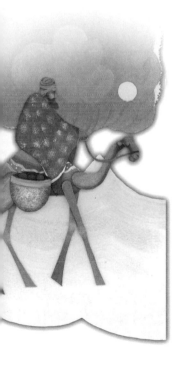

## 296

Father God, may we this Christmas-time:
make room for you with the innkeeper,
sing with the angels,
rejoice with the shepherds,
seek you with the wise men
and worship you as Lord and king.

MARION THOMAS

297 We cannot see what things are ahead of us.
Some will be good things, some will be bad things.
Help us to thank you for the good things,
trust you if things are hard for us,
and ask for your help whatever happens.

RHONA DAVIES

298
May this new year
be a new beginning for our family,
dear Father God.

LEWIS, AGED 6

299
Thank you for a new start!
Thank you for so many things
to look forward to!

STEPHEN, AGED 7

300 Yesterday, today and for ever,
Jesus is the same!

BASED ON HEBREWS 13:8

301

New opportunities,
New possibilities,
Things unseen and unknown,
Give me faith to step out into this new year, Lord,
Knowing that you are always with me.

MARION THOMAS

302

It's a whole new year today, God!
What will happen this year?
There'll be birthdays and special days,
schooldays and holidays,
happy days and sad days,
rainy days and sunny days.
Lots of days to work and play,
and you've given me each new day
to wake up and say: 'Thank you, God!'

JAN GODFREY

### 303

Lord, one day everyone loved you.
Then suddenly your friends left you,
and betrayed you
and denied they even knew you.
Then people shouted for your death.
Then they let you die, alone and in pain.
Thank you for suffering all that for me.

JONATHAN WILLIAMS

304 Jesus, it must have hurt so much
to be crucified.
I don't want to think about it.

PETER, AGED 6

305 Lord Jesus,
thank you for dying on a cross
so that all the bad things I do
can be forgiven.

MARION THOMAS

## 306

Lord Jesus, today is called Good Friday
and it's a very sad, dark day.
I'll remember how your enemies
(and even one of your friends) betrayed you.
I'll remember too that you died on a wooden cross
in lots of pain because you loved the world so much.
I'll remember your outstretched arms.
I'll remember how the sun went in,
and the sky became black,
and everywhere was still and very, very quiet.
I'll remember you, Lord Jesus.
Please remember me always.

JAN GODFREY

## 307

Dear Father God,
Jesus became a servant to teach us how to love,
and died on a cross so that we might live.
Help me to put other people first
and to think about their needs before my own.

RHONA DAVIES

308 Lord Jesus, you're alive again,
the stone has rolled away!
Let's all shout, 'Alleluia!'
because it's Easter Day!

JAN GODFREY

309

To him who has loved me,
and saved me from sin,
be glory for ever and ever, amen.

FROM EPHESIANS 3:20–21

310

You are here, Lord.
You are risen from the dead
And you are my Lord.
Let everyone know that you are real, Lord,
That you are my Lord,
That you are here, Lord.

JONATHAN WILLIAMS

311 Thank you, Lord Jesus,
   that you rose from the dead
   so that I can one day live with you in heaven.
   Thank you, Lord Jesus!

SALLY ANN WRIGHT

312

Thank you, Lord Jesus,
that the sadness of your cruel death
on Good Friday has a happy ending!

BETHAN JAMES

313 Jesus, you're alive!
   Once only a few friends could see you and talk to you
   but now I can and my friends can
   and everyone can!

MARY, AGED 7

314 May God who clothes the lilies of the field,
and feeds the birds of the sky,
who leads the lambs to pasture
and guides the deer to water,
clothe us, feed us, lead us and guide us,
and change us to be more like our loving Creator.

TRADITIONAL

315 Thank you, Lord, at harvest-time,
for sending rain and sunshine
to make the plants grow.
Thank you for the farmers
who cut the grain;
for the millers who make the flour;
for the bakers who bake the bread;
for the shopkeepers who sell our food.
Thank you, Lord, for all your gifts to us.

SALLY ANN WRIGHT

316 For farmers and tractors
and seedtime and harvest,
thank you, Lord.

SCOTT, AGED 6

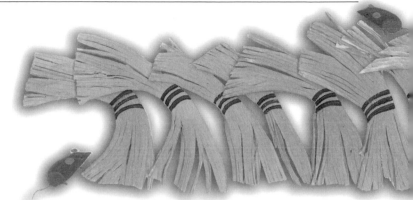

**317**

Praise God,
who gives the sun and rain,
and swells the grain,
that makes our bread
and keeps us fed.

TRADITIONAL

**318**

Thank you, God,
for a good harvest.
Thank you for food to eat,
some to keep, and some to
share.

TRADITIONAL

319 I can't wait to go on holiday, God!
We're going to be by the sea!
(P.S. I will miss home just a little bit.)

REBECCA, AGED 5

320 School's out—yippee!
Come and play, God,
and join in our games—it's
bucket and spade time,
swim in the sea time,
ride on a plane time,
flying a kite time,
swing in the park time,
staying up late time,
lots of ice cream time,
fun in the sun time,
reading a book time,
thank you God time!

JAN GODFREY

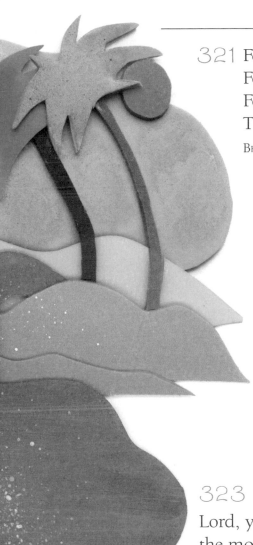

321 For salty sea and sunny skies,
For walks in mountains and hillsides,
For time to rest and time to play,
Thank you, God, for my holiday.

BETHAN JAMES

322

Please, Lord,
look after us on our journey.
Bless us and protect us
so that we arrive safely.

SALLY ANN WRIGHT

323

Lord, you made the sea and sand,
the mountains and hillsides,
the sun and the snow.
Thank you that we are going on holiday.

MARION THOMAS

**324** Father God, thank you for my family.
Thank you when we can be on holiday
and do fun things together.

HOLLY, AGED 6

**325** Lord God,
who never slumbers or sleeps,
bless us as we go out
and keep us safe as we return,
now and always.

BASED ON PSALM 121

**326** God the Father,
please keep me in your care;
Lord Jesus, be my constant friend;
Holy Spirit, guide me in all I do.
Bless me and protect me
until I come safely
to the end of my journey.

ADAPTED FROM A TRAVELLER'S BLESSING

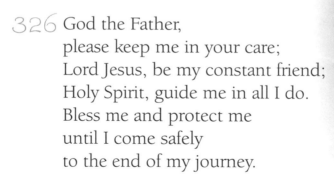

### 327

Creator God, Lord of all the world,
Thank you for new places to see,
different scenery, different faces,
different food and different spaces,
time to spend with people we love,
and time to make new friends.
Creator God, Lord of all the world,
thank you.

SALLY ANN WRIGHT

### 328

Splashy sea,
Big blue sky,
Shiny stones,
Grasses tall.
Trickling sand,
Knobbly shells...
Thank you, God!
You made it all.

SALLY ANN WRIGHT

## 329

Thank you, Lord Jesus, for special times,
like parties and weddings and celebrations.
We know you are our special guest,
who's there with us sharing the fun.

JAN GODFREY

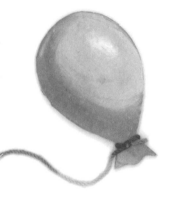

## 330

It's my birthday party today, God!
I'm scared and nervous and excited
because today is my special day.
Please make everything go well.

LLOYD, AGED 7

## 331

For this new morning and its light,
For rest and shelter of the night,
For health and food, for love and friends,
For every gift your goodness sends,
Thank you, gracious Lord.

TRADITIONAL

## 332

Nice things to eat and special clothes to wear,
thank you for good times and fun times
and time to see people we haven't seen for a while.
If something does go wrong,
help us not to get cross or too upset
but to share it with each other and with you.

SALLY ANN WRIGHT

## 333

Thank you for good things to eat and drink.
Thank you for happiness and laughter
and friends and family.
Thank you for all the good things you give us!

BETHAN JAMES

334 Look at my new baby, God!
So tiny and perfect—with such teeny hands and feet
and a sleepy scrunched-up face.
Sometimes there's a lot of crying
and a lot of milk and a lot of nappies
and my mum's really busy
and hasn't quite so much time to play with me.
But there's enough cuddles for everyone.
I really do love my new baby very much,
and I know you do too. Thank you, God!

JAN GODFREY

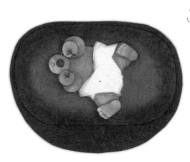

335 Thank you, heavenly Father,
that you made me,
that you made my family,
that you made this new tiny baby.
Bless and take care of our baby now.

SALLY ANN WRIGHT

336 Creator God, you are the giver of all good things
and you have given us a baby.
Thank you for the wonder of this new life.
Thank you for this miracle, this gift of a child.

MARION THOMAS

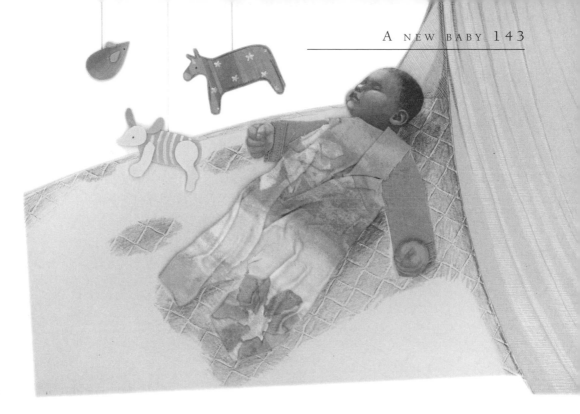

## 337

Thank you
for making
my Auntie Chris
have baby Eric.

MELEK-MARY, AGE 5

## 338

Thank you, Father God,
for the wonder and mystery of new life.
Watch over and protect this child
and bless our family with love,
strength and understanding,
so that we can take care of our new baby.

JONATHAN WILLIAMS

## 339

Now I lay me down to sleep,
I pray the Lord my soul to keep:
May God guard me through the night
And wake me with the morning light.

TRADITIONAL

## 340

Our Father God,
help us to know you are holy;
help us to be so kind to other people
that this world is like heaven.
Please give everyone enough to eat,
and forgive us for the things we've done
to hurt each other.
Help us not to do bad things,
and keep us safe with you always.

BASED ON MATTHEW 6:9–13

341

Angel of God, my guardian dear,
To whom God's love commits me here,
Every night be at my side,
To light and guard
To rule and guide.

TRADITIONAL

342

Into your hands, Lord,
I commit myself tonight.
Let angels surround my bed,
and peaceful thoughts
be always in my head.

BASED ON A PRAYER FROM UGANDA

343 Be near me, Lord Jesus,
I ask you to stay
Close by me for ever
And love me, I pray.
Bless all the dear children
In your tender care
And take us to heaven
To live with you there.

ANON.

344 Into your loving care,
Into your keeping,
You who are everywhere,
Take us, we pray.

TRADITIONAL

345 Creator God who made me,
Creator God who loves me,
Creator God who cares for me,
Keep me safe tonight.

SALLY ANN WRIGHT

346

From ghoulies and ghosties
And long-legged beasties
And things that go bump in the night,
Good Lord, deliver us.

A SCOTTISH PRAYER

347 Here I am, Lord, saying my prayers.
Thank you for all the things I did today
for the friends I saw and the things I had to eat.
Oh yes, and sorry for making my room a mess.
I made Mum upset.

TOM, AGED 7

## 348

Stay with me,
Father God, for it is evening,
and the day is coming to an end.
Stay with me and all those I love,
in the evening of this day,
now and in eternity.

TRADITIONAL

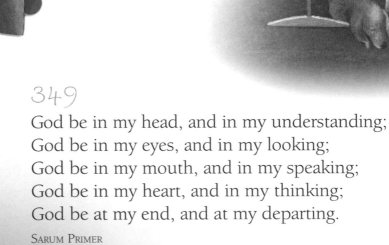

## 349

God be in my head, and in my understanding;
God be in my eyes, and in my looking;
God be in my mouth, and in my speaking;
God be in my heart, and in my thinking;
God be at my end, and at my departing.

SARUM PRIMER

## 350

In my little bed I lie:
heavenly Father, hear my cry;
Lord, keep me safe throughout this night.
Wake me up at morning light.

ANON.

## 351

Before the end of the day,
Creator of the world, we pray
that you, with steadfast love, would keep
your watch around us while we sleep.

BASED ON THE ANGLICAN TRADITION

352 Lord, I know that you are near,
in darkness and in light.
You are always there,
to hear my prayer
and care for me tonight.

BETHAN JAMES

353 O God, you turn our world into darkness
and return it again to light.
Please watch over us now and keep us safe,
for you alone can take care of us
and you alone can bring us lasting peace.

TRADITIONAL

354

In the deep, dark, silent night,
Lord, we pray,
look kindly upon us
and keep us safe from danger,
for the sake of your Son, Jesus.

SUE DOGGETT

355 May God give us a quiet night,
and at the last, a perfect end;
and the blessing of God Almighty,
Father, Son, and Holy Spirit,
be with us this night and evermore.

A PRAYER FROM CANADA

## 356

Angels bless and angels keep,
angels guard me while I sleep.
Bless my heart and bless my home,
bless my spirit as I roam.
Guide and guard me through the night
and wake me with the morning's light.

TRADITIONAL

## 357

Please God,
Bless me when I'm walking,
Bless me when I'm talking,
Bless me when I'm playing,
Bless me when I'm praying,
Bless me when I'm eating,
Bless me when I'm sleeping.
Please bless me every minute
Of the day and night.

CHRISTINE WRIGHT

## 358

At the first light of sun:
God bless you.
When the long day is done:
God bless you.
In your smiles and in your tears:
God bless you.
Through each day of your years:
God bless you.

ADAPTED FROM AN IRISH BLESSING

## 359

God bless all those that I love;
God bless all those that love me;
God bless all those that love those that I love
and all those that love those that love me.

FROM A NEW ENGLAND SAMPLER

## 360

Watch over me, Father God, and bless me.
Help me to love all that is good and true,
and to be a blessing to others I meet.

BETHAN JAMES

## 361

God the Father keep us in his care,
the Lord Jesus Christ be our constant friend,
and the Holy Spirit guide us in all we do.

A TRAVELLER'S BLESSING

## 362

May the grace of Christ
our Saviour,
and the Father's boundless love,
with the Holy Spirit's favour
rest upon us from above.

JOHN NEWTON

## 363

May the Lord bless us and watch over us.
May the Lord make his face shine upon us
and be gracious to us,
may the Lord look kindly on us
and give us peace;
and the blessing of God almighty,
the Father, the Son, and the Holy Spirit,
be with us and remain with us now and every day.

BASED ON NUMBERS 6:24–26

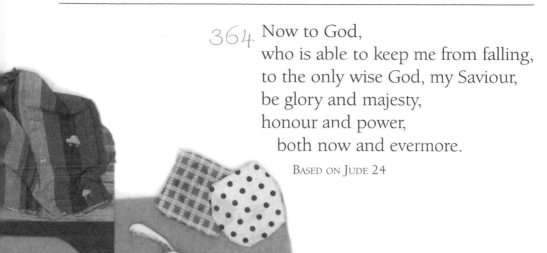

**364** Now to God,
who is able to keep me from falling,
to the only wise God, my Saviour,
be glory and majesty,
honour and power,
both now and evermore.

BASED ON JUDE 24

**365**

May God greatly bless us with his kindness;
with fresh, flowing waters of kindness.
May God greatly bless us with his peace;
with still, quiet waters of peace.
May God greatly bless us with his love;
with deep, thirst-quenching waters of love
now and always.

BASED ON JUDE 3

# Index of themes

The prayer numbers below will help you to find prayers about many different subjects.